LET'S ROLL

BRAVE HEARTS

By

J.J. BHATT

ISBN:

9798780046103

Title:

Let's Roll:
Brave Hearts

Author:

J.J. Bhatt

Published and Distributed by Amazon and Kindle worldwide.

This book is manufactured in the Unites States of America.

Recent Books
By J.J. Bhatt

(Available from Amazon)

HUMAN ENDEAVOR: *Essence & Mission/ A Call for Global Awakening, (*2011)

ROLLING SPIRITS: *Being Becoming* /A Trilogy, (2012)

ODYSSEY OF THE DAMNED: *A Revolving Destiny,* (2013).

PARISHRAM: *Journey of the Human Spirits*, (2014).

TRIUMPH OF THE BOLD: *A Poetic Reality*, (2015).

THEATER OF WISDOM, (*2016).*

MAGNIFICENT QUEST: *Life, Death & Eternity,* (2016).

ESSENCE OF INDIA: *A Comprehensive Perspective,* (2016).

ESSENCE OF CHINA: *Challenges & Possibilities*, (2016).

BEING & MORAL PERSUASION: *A Bolt of Inspiration*, (2017).

REFELCTIONS, RECOLLECTIONS & EXPRESSIONS, (2018).

ONE, TWO, THREE... ETERNITY: *A Poetic Odyssey, (*2018).

INDIA: *Journey of Enlightenment*, (2019a).

SPINNING MIND, SPINNING TIME: *C'est la vie*, (2019b).Book 1.

MEDITATION ON HOLY TRINITY, *(2019c), Book 2.*

ENLIGHTENMENT: *Fiat lux*, (2019d), Book 3.

BEING IN THE CONTEXTUAL ORBIT: *Rhythm, Melody & Meaning, (*2019e).

QUINTESSENCE: *Thought & Action,* (2019f).

THE WILL TO ASCENT: *Power of Boldness & Genius,* (2019g).

RIDE ON A SPINNING WHEEL: *Existence Introspected, (*2020a).

A FLASH OF LIGHT: *Splendors, Perplexities & Riddles,* (2020b).

ON A ZIG ZAG TRAIL: *The Flow of Life*, (2020c).

UNBOUNDED: *An Inner Sense of Destiny* (2020d).

REVERBERATIONS: The *Cosmic Pulse,* (2020e).

LIGHT & DARK: *Dialogue and Meaning,* (2021a).

ROLLING REALITY: *Being in flux, (2021b).*

FORMAL SPLENDOR: *The Inner Rigor,* (2021c).

TEMPORAL TO ETERNAL: *Unknown Expedition,* (2021d).

TRAILBLAZERS: *Spears of Courage*, (2021e).

TRIALS & ERRORS: *A Path to Human Understanding*, (2021f).

MEASURE OF HUMAN EXPERIENCE: *Brief Notes,* (2021g).

BEING BECOMING, (2022a)

INVINCIBLE, (2022b).

VALIDATION: *The Inner Realm of Essence*, (2022c).

LET'S ROLL: *Brave Hearts,* (2022d).

LIFE: *An Ellipsis, (2022e).*

THE CODE: *Destiny* (2022f).

PREFACE

Let's Roll: *Brave Hearts* is directional
as it encourages young generation to take a
bold stand and walk with an open-mind to
define a meaningful common destiny of the
world and be worthy of their inherited
moral courage and determined will. It is
also a reminder to the young that *time is of
the essence* to meet their individual
responsibility to realize the noble mission
as stated.

                                    J.J. Bhatt

CONTENTS

Once Upon

A thought,
Landing on,
"Once upon"

Not knowing
What would be
The response

Gently,
I knocked
Her door while
Holding onto my
Deep breath

Every sec
Seemed eternity
And suddenly, the
Door flung opened;
Bringing all lost
Memories alive

She stood
Face to face with
That beauty, that light,
That sweet smile and

The narrow
Gap of
"Now and then"
Vanished,
Instantaneously!

Big
Challenge

Beauty,
Justice
And fortitude
All for the
Noble good

While
Human seems
Buried into the
Shifting sands of
His time

What a
Blowing dust
Storm driven
By vanity full of
False narratives
And pseudo claims

There's an
Urgency to escape
From the
Stubborn darkness
To save the
Future of our kids...

Power of Love

As life,
Is a miracle
Of courage and
Big dream to
Seek

Let every
Being be a
Determined will
And begin
To rethink his/her
Role in the
Grand scheme of
All things

Let
Each leave
His/her own
Eternal poem full
Of deep feelings:
To be in love,
In love and in love
Forever...

Awakening

Decay and
Death,
Is it what we
Want
Our common
Destiny to be!

Let's
Go after the
Meaning of life
And start walking
Along a right track

Or else,
Decay and
Moral death
Always
The recurring
Theme of men;
Inflicted by the
Glorious blunders
And sins...

Remember

"Wisdom
Always a
Necessity"
To live well

And we can
Say "Being
Alone is the
Definer of the
Set mission" for

His soul is the
Inspiration
To act with a
Sincerity of
Purpose"

Indeed
Human
Got the power
To shape the
World the way
He dreams

But
Never forget,
Reality has its
Price called the
Moral commitment,
In return...

Resilient

It's a
Million layer
That shields him
Against constant
Conflicts and
Contradictions
Of his time

Often,
History
Reduces him to
Nothingness, but
Got the magic to
Bounce back
Every time

That's the
Miracle of the
Illumined beings
Ensuring stability
From one generation
To another and
The bold journey
Continues,
Terra firma alright...

Awakened

When the
Worlds turning
Material and
Very techno by
The minutes

Awakening
Is the solemn
Experience to
Escape the cage

Let him
Enrich the
Spiritual essence
For that's where
He shall have
The real freedom

Let him
Seek
Some balance
On the scene

Let him
Discover,
"Where Hope,
Harmony and
Happiness resides."

The
Way

Heroes are
Born from
Humanity
Alone

God is
Born in the
Human mind
Only

That's the
Truth to be
Understood
By the rational
Being today

Ideas
Too are born
From the inner
Spirit; defining
What is right or
What is not?

And
That's the
Ethical journey
We've been on
For a while..

Misplaced

Please
Don't torture
The little
Guy for a
Petite err

I say,
"Go catch the
Big boys;
Stealing our
Privacy and
Killing the
Identity,
Every time"

Ordinary
Folks seek
Peace only and
To see a secured
Future for their kids

Please
Don't let the greedy
Few keep exploiting
Children's dream...

Move-on

Didn't we
Survive the
Killer storm
Alright or not!

Now it's time
To move on
Where
Peace and
Goodwill is the
Social norm

Yes, yes
Let's evolve
To a point
Where we can
See our collective
Success in this
World

Come folks,
Time
To move on
To be,
"Better us..."

State of
Mind

Let every
Being fire-up:
Zest, laughter
And love
While riding
Through the time

If we
Keep going the
Right direction
There is Gloria,
Harmony and Joy
Shall be our
Best friends

Let the
Inner being
Spark: zest,
Laughter and
Meaning while
Riding through the
Turbulent time...

Nebulous

The other
Many realities
Beyond conception
We shall never know

That's the
Eternal blindside
Of us finite alright

What if,
The journey
After death
Be the only
Way!

Is it the
Hidden
Meaning
To keep all
Intelligent minds
Busy forever in
The name called,
"Truth!"

Freedom

In the very
Act of making
Choices,
We exercise
Our
Individual
"Freewill"
Indeed

That is the
Moment, we're
The master of
Our destiny and
Nothing else

That is
When we
Make things,
Events and
Experiences to
Happen, but face
The consequences
At the same time too...

Gist

While
Seeking the
Meaning of
His moral self
Being is caught
In the never
Ending drama of
The good and evil

If he's
On the
Wrong side,
He is in the
Grip of misery,
Pain and despair

If he's
Smart,
He'll know,
"His moral
Courage" and
Overcome all the
Ugly experiences
In the end...

Being & Meaning

Feelings
Sparkling
With meaning
Keeps existence
Steady on the
Set course

When
The soul is
Illuminated;
All is but the
Beautiful Bliss

That's the
Goal
That's the
Direction
Let it be
The essence of
Human existence...

Chin-up

Let's
Learn,
"How to save
Our dignity"
Under every
Pressing
Situation

Let's
Ascend to
The highest
Realm
Where
We're
The total
Significant

Let's
Get the best
From each

Let's
Be the mighty
Inspiration
To the young...

Justification

We're
The reality
Justifying to
Be alive today

Yes,
We're born
To enhance the
Global Hope and
Harmony at last

Let it be
The meaning of
Our collective
Worthiness

Let it be
The future
Where kids shall
Grow up with
Such a noble spirit

Let it
Be our collective
Responsibility
To define a good
World of tomorrow
While being alive today...

Missing
Identity

Human Mind,
What a
Wonderful
Abstractive:
Thinking, feeling,
Machine always
In quest to grasp,
Totality-of- all-
Experience

Being
Standing alone
Against all odds and
Seeking to awaken
The dormant Spirit
To understand,
"What is it all about?"

Being,
Weary of
His tribal belief
And afraid to reform
Well,
That is where
He must begin the
Magnificent quest
As his first step...

Illumined

Each
An illumined
Soul, albeit
A spirit
That's ready in
Lifting others to
The highest peak

Each
A great value
To his/her birth
Each
Always a light
In every dark place

That's
The very meaning
Of being born in
Human form and
That is the essence
To be grasped well...

Great
Ride

Let
Creative
Thoughts be
The chariot;
Riding us
To perfection
By the sec

And, let
The power of
Intuition
Show us the
Right way

Let us
Learn,
"How
To keep the
Ride steady
And smooth and
Let it
Run its course...

Celebration

While
On the
Highway
To the
Self-discovery

Who
Knows?
What's the
Meaning of
*Totality-of-all
-That-is'*

Perhaps
It's just another
Invention of the
Human mind,
Essentially

Who
Knows?
How far do
We've got to be
The simplicity of
Our thoughts only

In the big
Picture,
"why not celebrate
Our births, our joint
Destiny...our dream
In the total harmony,
All That Is!

Be Brave

As you
Keep walking
Along the trail
Think
Not of the
Limited time,
But eternity being
The real friend

As you
Keep evolving
Through the
Spiritual knowing
Think
Not of the
Tribe, but the
Good of the
Whole

Learn
How to rise
Above triviality
And stick to the
Set noble goals
And don't ask,
"Why?"But think,
"Why not?"

Take
Charge

Shape the
World with your
Will and dream
As you wish it
To be

If you
Don't like it
Then relearn,
"How to change
In time"

If you
Want peace
And hope to
Rule the world

Be ready
To roll-up the
Sleeves and quit
The old habits:
Bigotry, violence
And greed...

Inspiration

Struggling
Humans
Facing the strong
Winds of change
Keeps running to
Save their souls

In such
Uncertain
Reality,
Let 'em
Pause and
Reinvigorate
Their
Inner Being

Let 'em
Stir up the
Raging freewill
And let it
Strength their
Moral being...

Belief
Vs Faith

Faith is pure,
Eternal and
Internal essence
With no insistence
To worship any
Brand name

Belief
Is organized,
Temporal and
Often corrupt

Faith is
Freedom while
Belief demands
Obedience to the
Stringent rules

Faith is
Rational and
Inclusive, but
Belief seems tribal
And often exclusive

Faith is
Moral strength
And rational for it is
Driven by the noble spirit,
Called, "The Inner Will"

The Link

Human and
Dream
Seems deeply
Woven by the
Very fabric of the
Great expectations

In reality,
Ambiguity of
Existence keeps
'Em often
In conflict and

That's
The troublesome
Drama riding him
Through time
After time and
He never
Tries hard to get
Off the grip

Dream and
Reality,
What an unintended
Consequence,
"What he wishes and
What he receives in the
End is not necessarily
The same experience."

Why
Chaos

Funny,
What
We see and
What others see
The same, but
We deduce it
Differently

I mean,
What we say
And what others
Hear may not
Carry the same
Meaning

Albeit,
What
The story is and
What the reader
Absorbs its essence
May not be
The same thing!

Hello Reality!

Often I
Wonder,
"What is my
Real essence in
This mighty but
Dying Universe"

Hello
Reality
Are you still
With me and
Respecting my
Quest to find the
Teasing truth

Is it
A wishful
Thinking or am I
Missing something
Beyond awareness
Or my inner spirit?

Wonder
If 'am just
A Stream of
Consciousness
To affirm,
"All that is simply
The subjective
Judgment of my
Thought only..."

Power
To Be

Each a
Very essence
Born to write
His/her story

Each an
Adventure
Rolling with
Full confidence

Each a
Very moral
Adding value
To humanity
In return

Each a
Creative gift
Being worthy
Of his own birth...

Echoes

The
Orwellian
Ghost is
Knocking the
World, today

It's,
"How to
Manipulate
Human thoughts
Every
Whichever way"

If lies
Repeated over
And again,
Oddly turns into
"Truth"
And "Slavery"
To "Freedom"

Beware of
The Orwellian
Prophecy
As the
Ignorant minds
Are easy prey
To many culprits,
Today...

Dear Mother

Mother of
Invention led us
From caves to the
Agro experience

Mama also
Reared us with
Belief of
Different flavors,
But we
Failed to know
Its significance

Well
Darkness
Gripped the world
And blood spilled
Over long

Today,
Mother gave
A beautiful gift,
"Techno Elixir"

But it seems,
We're silently
Fading from the
Scene as our
Identity and dignity
Have been renamed,
"Numbers, codes and
Categories for sure..."

Divine Vision

It's
Not others
To dictate,
"How
We've to be"

Its' the
Self judgment
To save our
Dignity each
Time

While
Pursuing truth
Let not others
Tell, "What to do
Or what not to"

That's
The Freedom
We must guard
At each time

While
Walking
Through the
Thick and thin
Patch...

Long Journey

What
We believe
Is the mental
Construct
Only

Whats
To be
Understood
Is power
Of the spirit
Within

Whats
To be
Explored is
"Truth"

Whats
To be
Gifted is
"Pure silence
Of the soul..."

Unfinished Mission

Being
An amazing
Thought churning
Machine caught in
His changing times

He's
Fallen to the
Abyss of
Hedonism and
War-mongering
Habits and

Keeps
Walking with
Obsession of
Freedom without
Responsibility;
Killing all his
Big dreams...

What
If

Search
For
Truth means
"Self-discovery"

And that's
The prime game
We must play
Before we're
No more

It's only
One-way to
Fulfill the set
Mission

It's
The only
Reason to know,
"Who we're and
What we can
Become"

At the Edge

Let
Every being
Be an ever
Creative
Wonderer
In this
Reality of
The Light and
Dark Cosmos

In this
Vast
Throbbing
Fiery Universe

Let him
Dare probe into
The notions
Of God,
Contradictions
And paradoxes

I mean,
With a clarity
Of his
Rational insight...

A Ride

We've
Been
Riding high
For a very long

Yes,
We've been
On a destiny
That we don't
Know it so well

At times,
Future seems
More of a
Nemesis than
A friend

Such is the
Story of each
Generation and
The error to be
Corrected at
Each time...

Forlorn

Being
Forlorn,
What a terrible
Experience to
Encounter

It's
State of the
Mind perhaps
Victim of own
Exclusiveness,
Or what!

That's
Been the
Plight of those
Caught into a
War-torn zone

We're
Guilty
Every time
I mean,
For neglecting
Fellow
Dear humans
Who've lost their
Hope and dream...

On the
Go

What if
Dream is the
Beginning and
Reality is but
An endless pursuit
Of every human

What if
Disorder is the
First cause and
The order is the
Consequence
While humans
Keep swinging
Between rights
And wrongs

Why don't
Humans sustain
Their collective
Dream and order
For the good of the
Whole?

Dark
Side

Negative
Forces keeps
Reducing human
To be nothing

Beware,
Ignorance,
Arrogance and
False narratives
Could erase,
"What He is"

That is,
How he can
Turn into
A permanent
Insignificant
By every
Measuring stick...

Reflection

It's
The flow
From self-love
To the selfless
Love

Let it be
The hidden
Theme of
Human essence

If this
Simple
Equation is
Understood well

There
Shall be Heaven
On Earth and
We shall be free
In the true sense

Indeed
If fully liberated
We shall redefine
Ourselves and

There will be
No necessity to
Worship, but to
Keep walking
Along the
Right track...

Confrontation

Why
No place left
To meditate for
A brief

Why
No peace
To the modern
Being at all

Is it
All about
Wealth, power
And fame and
Neglect of the
Beautiful bliss...

Hope
That Is

Where
There is an
Awakened
Being
There's
Eternal light,
Always

When
Human acts
Upon his dream
He has
Began the walk

Yes, when
He realizes
He's the
Inspiration
To the young

That's the
Turning point
That's the
Enlightenment
In action alright...

Our Issues

Let's not
Retreat
Let's not
Even think
To quit

Our main
Issue,
"How to
Stay focus with
The mission at
All time"

Another
Pressing issue,
"How to be free
From the fear of
Death"

Let's
Welcome Death,
What is our
Continued
Journey beyond

Yes,
To experience
Deeper meaning,
"Being born in
The human form."

Watch Out!

When
We gaze
At the countless
Stars smiling
In the stygian
Night

Remember,
All is so brief.
All so ephemeral
And all is nothing
But uncertainty
In the end

Don't
Wait but
Keep walking
Through the
Starlight

Don't worry
The stygian night
Shall rule the
Terrain 'til the
Early dawn...

The
Drive

Into the
Total Reality
Where all
Happenings is
Constant conflict

And to this
Intelligent being;
All he's just creating
Short time opinions and
Never standing still

Albeit
There is no
Puzzle over here,
But whatever it is,
Remains beyond
His perception

All queries
Shall endure
Forever so long
He's caged into
The rigid machine of
Conceptual thinking...

A Paradox

Being
Simple,
Yet
So complex
That's the
Paradox
Yet to be
Deciphered

Though
Being is the
Light all that is
Why
He remains
Now and then
In the dark

And being,
A power of
Good,
Why is he
The cause and
Consequence of
Million blood spills!

A Measure

When
Circumference
Divided by the
Radius
There is the
Reality called,
The value of Pie

When
Infinite is
Divided by
The finites,
Only Infinity
Remains forever

Human
Just an
Insignificant
Spark; nothing
To prove, but
What a miracle

What a sweet
Pie of infinity in
The finite Universe...

Gusto

Hey, hey
My friends,
"Is there a
Chance to be
Heroes in our
Time"

Yes, I am
Asking again,
"Is there a
Way to be
Heroes of the
Time"

Hey there
Brave hearts,
Are you ready?
To ride the
Big dream today
Or not"

Hey, hey
Dear world,
Are you ready?
To roll forward
With Good in your
Heart or not!

Effervesces

It's
Definitely
A short walk
Between
Life and death
And time is
Slipping away
So fast

It's
Certainly
A realm of
"New" every
Now and then

Where every
Beings
Caught by the
World of rapid
Change

What if
All human
Endeavors
End up but
*Harmony and
Peace...*

Be
Alert

Grasp, but
Don't fail to
Introspect,
"For you're
An expression of
The sacred soul"

Don't
Ignore, but try
To understand,
"For you're
A rational being,
Indeed"

Be
Fearless
Always and
Hold on to your
Awakened turf,
"For you're the
Walker heading
Toward your
Own Truth"

Life

Life
What a brief
Moment to
Cherish:

A few dreams,
Million
Memories and
Some sweet and
Sour experiences

Life
What
We make
Of it with the
Power of the will

Life
What a
Slippery
Slope, if not
Checked with
Right awareness

Life
What an
Inspiring source
To the temporal
Intelligent beings...

Being & Essence

Into this
Revolving
Mass
Confusions

How shall
We build
Moral strength
To fulfill our
Waiting dreams

Yes,
That's the
The journey of
Our meaning
That we've been
After

And that's the
Measure of our
Collective sincerity
To meet the pending
Challenge today....

Image

Our
Infinite
Exuberance
Must be
Hidden strength;
Flying us to the
Sanctum of truth
Itself

Our
Efflorescent
Bliss let it be
The norm in
The times to
Come

Our
Divine Soul,
Let it be the
Determined
Will dare to
Go beyond the
Turbulences of
Our time...

Tribute

On the
First glance at
Goliath,
Young David
Confidently
Uttered,
"I can take him"

He
Catapulted
A sharp pebble
And killed
The giant on
The spot and
It was all a
Brief moment

Yes,
It was one
Young brave,
Redefining
Courage before
The world and

Let it
Be a perennial
Inspiration
To the young
Everywhere...

It's
Ticking

**Human
Burdened by
Arrogance,
Power and
Big fame**

**Yet taking
A nose-dives;
Disintegrating
Into million pieces
Of nothing in time**

**It has
Happened before,
Its happening
Today and shall
Happen tomorrow**

**Revenge,
Greed and
Narcissism and
Many more
Those humans
What a nasty
Time-ticking
Bombs!**

World
Song

Come
Folks and let's
Sing together,
"Who we're
And what we
Can become"

Yes, folks
Let's keep the
Chin-up and
Find the way,
"How to be
Strong"

Let's
Live life with a
Roaring courage
And be free forever

Come on
Folks let's lit
Inspire the
Young braves

Let's
Hand over the
Torch and
Let 'em roll the
World to their
Big dream...

Turning
Point

Remember
These great
Turning points:
1215, 1776, 1789,
1947 and many
More

Each
A historic date of
Moral triumph
When people
Secured ideals of
Freedom, Justice
And Equality...
All hall marks of
Democracy

That has been
The independent
Spirit of every
Human from the
Beginning

It's time,
Today once again
To demand, ""We're
Not numbers to be fed
Into giga-data banks
We're
Indeed, humans
With names, dignity and
Humanity in us always"

Silent
Truth

What love,
Means we
Never knew

What
Promise we
Made not
So obvious ever

That is how
We've
Endured
Through the
Years

Only love
Kept us
Together
And separate
At the same time

That's been
The unexplained
Magic we never
Understood so well...

Validation

Every
Single born is
A flashing hope
To the whole

Every
Single turn is
A giant leap
Forward of all

Every
Single child,
What a
Brilliant star
That shall shine
For sure

Come,
Let us
Celebrate
Life as is and

Let us
Make best of
It while
The ride is on
For sure...

Rear View

Fly
Thought to
The high hills
Of once upon

Where
Fresh air and
Clean waters
Gave us inner
Strength

Our
Diet was
Natural and
Family talked
Daily at the
Dinner table,
Alright

Life
Then was
Hard, but real
Humanity was
The strength

Well here
We're today
Where techno-
Cousins are slowly
Began to control our
Thoughts, our
Dignity and even
Our humanity
Indeed...

Historic
Law

When
World is at the edge
That's when real action
Begins and things change

Yes,
That's the grand story
Of our kind from the
Very inception

As dark
Clouds hover over
Our heads that's when
Collectively, we angrily
Demand change

And it is
A short-time deal each
Time and the cycle repeats
Over and again...

Keep
Walking

**Human,
Must be
The biggest
Agent of
Social
Corruption**

**In that
Case, he
Alone must
Reform his
Old habits and**

**Regain
The real
Meaning of
His freedom**

**Neither the
Divine nor the
Saints can help
Only he must
Resolve the
Challenge on
His own.**

Ethical
Will

When
Humanity
Suffers from
Myopia, phobia
And distrust
Do us really
Know,
"How to heal the
Deep wound"

Is it the
Consequence
Of our mental
Confusions or
False narratives
That set the stage
Or what?

"Is it
Why our quest
Of freedom, justice,
And equality remains
But a mirage and the
Journey seems too long!

Time
Tower

Why while
Travels through
Life, we're being
Thrown off the
Track many times

Is it a
Recurring
Experience
Those seeking
To walk all the
Way to the
Temple of Truth

Is it
'Cause being
Is caught by the
Swirling winds of
His ethical dilemma
May be!

Sophia

Sophia was
A feisty old lady
In her eighties
Who possessed
Worldly wisdom
Quite well

She told me
Her story of
Younger days and
Confessed,
"She was
Once a stubborn,
Querulous and
Ruthless bitch"

While
Collecting her
Thoughts and taking
Couple puffs from
The cigar she continued,
"I never hurt anyone,
But only the fake lovers"

She chuckled
And said, "Today I am
An awakened light and
Have absolved all my
Sins and now I am at peace"

Erratum!

When
We're
Hanging
Between the
Narrow thread
Called,
"Birth & Death"

How can we
Say, "I'm an
Individual and
Being free"

We may
Claim,
"We're
Separate
Individuals,
Yet, we're
Virtually we're
Contextual
Always"

Why such
A contradictory
Situation while
We're desperately
Seeking to honor our
Individual dignity!

Simplicity

If one is a
Noble Soul,
Why be too
Divinely crazy

In other
Words,
All that is
Necessary,
"How to walk
The walk"

In other
Words,
In the end,
Al that is
Necessary is

To be the
Illumined spirit
With one's own
Endeavor in the
Name of Good...

Tossed
Coin

In life,
Sometimes
We win and
Sometimes we
May not

In love,
Sometimes
We're
Lucky and
Sometimes
We may not

And that's
The game
We play life
After life

Love,
Life and
Laughter
Governing,
"Who we're,"
But the story
Never ends...

Think
Again

Verily,
The past is
A tall mount
Leading us to the
Present ever

In turn,
Present is
An arrow shot
Toward future
But that is
So unknown

In such
An uneasy
State of
Existence,
Humans
Searching for
Their own
Meaning and

Even
Children
Asking, "Well,
What about us?"

Doppelganger

To be
Simple and
Silent means,
You're the
Most beautiful
Indeed

Balancing
Equally
Between
Joy and grief
Means
You're the
Moral maturity
In action

Knowing,
You're the
Temporal
Ascending
To the eternal
Means, you've
Understood the
Self so well...

Sacred
Fire

Standing
Before the
Blazing pyre
And recollecting
Memories of the
Beloved who's
No more

Suddenly,
I saw her image
In the bellowing
Smokes as she
Waived the final
Goodbye

The priest
Kept chanting
But all seemed
So silent
As zephyr
From the east
Whispered through
The smoky memories;
Tears confessed,
"I'd loved her the most..."

Janus

Let
The young
Succeed in
New adventure
Where their
Elders failed

Let
The braves
Clean-up the
Mess left behind
By their elders

Yes, yes
Let 'em
Stand-up and
Criticize their
Elders while
They're still here...

Celestial

There is a
Distant star
Shining so
Brilliantly
Each night

Her name
Is Celeste and
She sings life
Full of rosy song
And big dream

Oh what
An inspiration
Shinning
In the vastness
Of the Unknown

She
Illuminate
All possibilities
She is a live
Courage and
A bold guidance
To go beyond...

Facade

Drop the
Man-made
Belief that's
Burdened by
Contradictions
And double-talks

Drop the
Mask of social
Etiquette; claiming
"You're
Better than others"

Let 'em
Hit the ground
When death says,
"Hello" in the end

Meanwhile
Let integrity of
The mind and
Rational intention
Guide you through
Life's imperfections
With full trust in
Your Moral Self...

Beware

Sorrow
Over human
Existence is an
Insufficient
Reason to begin the
Journey any time

If
No-action
Turns
Into a begnin
Social norm,
In that case,
Enlightenment
May not be
Coming soon

Be aware,
The winds of
Change can
Sweep away all
Waiting dreams

Be smart
And know,
"Where the
Trail's going..."

Being & Essence

Meditation
Not a
Metaphysical
Melodrama,
But a
Necessasity
To clarify the
Empirical errors

Again,
Introspection
Not an individual
Quest, but a
Grasp of the whole
Through silencing
The Mind

After all,
We're
The Totality of
All That Is, but
Must remain
Alert and calm
At the same time....

Illumination

It's been
Said, "Keep the
Plot, dialogues,
Actions and casts
Intricately well
Woven to give a
Story its master
Stroke"

Likewise,
Keep the drama
Of life intact with
Right vision and
Moral sensibility
To make it a master
Piece as well

Let each
Shape his/her
Time into a big
Story inspiring the
Young life after life...

Blinkers

Man and
Woman
Though
Two separate
Egos,
When in love,
They're one

Right or
Wrong always
In conflict
When
Second-hand
Opinions is the
Judge of it all

Hope and
Despair keeps
Colliding
When state
Of the mind is
Nebulous and
Blinded by a
False belief...

Power
To Be

Against
All odds,
Human still
Remains
The light in
This exploding
Universe

That's why
He's in control
Of his destiny
No matter what
May be the
Consequence

Human
Indeed a
Link between
Known and
Unknown
For he's all
Possibilities with
No limit to think of...

Unknown
Pal

He was a
Senior pal like
A big brother

He was
Good man and
Quiet one

Once he was
A business man
And enjoyed the
Luxury of life

He then
Became a
Priest and what
A changed
Human being
He was

Suddenly,
One day he
Withdrew from
The world and
Died silently
Telling no one,
"He was gone..."

The
Flow

What if,
There ain't an
Escape from
The chameleon
Social patterns
Woven into rough
And tough flows

What if,
Goodness fades
With time when
Too much noise
Fills the human
Spirit

What if,
Meditative
State of the mind
Insulates him from
His own evil habits
At every turning point...

Overture:
Life

Youth and
Innovation
Always high
Energy to note
Well

They're
The game
Changers and
Lifters of the
Awareness

Reason and
Moral courage
Always the
Provenance of
High hope and
Possibilities
To note well

Life
What a
One time gift
To be
Handled with
A deep sense of
Responsibility at
Each step ...

Note Well

If we
Refuse to
Know
The past,
We may not
Understand the
Present so well

And, if we
Fail to grasp
The urgency of
The present,
We may not
Reckon what the
Future may hold

In other
Words, if we
Keep walking
Through the dark
For a long

We may
Perish into chaos
And ignorance and
That would be,
"Our collective death..."

Formula

Life
What a
Consequence of
Thoughts, words
And choices

If the
Formula is
Right, it's a
Magic to the
Every heart

Love too
Simply an
Overture:
Feelings, trust
And friendship

If the
Formula is right,
It's also a magic
To the two beating
Hearts

Life
What a magic,
"How to
Balance all the
Feelings into
Right proportions...

Our
Challenge

Do you
Think children
Shall write their
Stories and
Relive in
Harmony with a
New Global Spirit

Do you
Vision
Tomorrow
Shall be more
Meaningful and
Progressive than
Today when looking
At the kids

And must
Honestly ask,
"What Have
We done enough
To keep the story
Inspiring for the
Children of today?"

The
Cage

There is
Always the
Struggle to
Know the Self
So well

There is
Always the
Ecstasy and
Agony of love

There is
Always this
Corrupted being
Walking along a
Tight rope of
To be good and his
Battle ain't over yet...

History
Speaks

When
Humanity
Plagued by the
Barrage of lies,
Fake news and
Distorted facts

That is
When soft
Death begins
To kill
Civility, morality
And dignity of
The human spirit

There were
Once
Great powers
Each so
Ambitious and
Had an efficient
War machines

Sadly,
Ignorance,
Arrogance and the
Disease of indifferent
Attitude killed their
Glory and dreams,
Each time...

Precious

Fair justice
Is the beam
Structure of
Every great
Society

If it's
Weakened,
Citizens
May not be
Free as they may
Otherwise feel

That's why,
Mighty important
To keep the structure
Strong and save the
Breath of democracy
At all time...

Look at the
Totalitarians,
They've imprisoned
Millions and denying
Their freedom

In their
Hellish world, there's
Only ruthlessness,
Arrogance and darkness...

Global
Voice

Let's declare
Our intention
Today:

We're
The spirits of
Courage and we're
Not afraid to change
The world for good

Come,
Let's sing the
Song that's an
Inspiration of all
Young braves

Come,
Let's be the
Friends and attain
The global issues
Of our time as one
Reverberating voice...

Core
Essence

**Let each
Understand,
We're not
Doing so well
Today**

**It's
Pertinent
To listen to one
Others while
Trying to be
Total humans**

**Let us
Continue in
Strengthening
Our collective
Determined Will
To make it through**

**Yes, as we
Pursue to be
Relevant in our
Own imperfections.**

Riders

As time
Keeps rolling
Like an aimless
Arrow shot
Through a dark
Terrain and
Going nowhere

We
Mustn't be
That arrow at
All for our times
Slipping away so
Swift

But we
Mustn't wait
Either 'till the
Last minute
To begin
The journey
Of our meaning

History is
Such a scenario
Where future is
Not known until
We're there
To experience it
The first-hand ...

1+ 1= 1

Life and
Nature
Two manifests of
One reality at the
Very core

Thought and
Action
Two connected
Adventures
Defining One
Human essence

Right and
Wrong
Two separate
Consequences
Of one judgment
In the end

Birth and
Death
Two distant dots,
But one reality
To experience

Lovers too
Are two separate
Hearts yet bounded
By one mighty trust...

Mirage

God, what a
Spectacular
Mirage born from
The human mind

Let humans
Be free from
Fear of the
Unknown and

Let 'em
Learn to
Be rational
To seek their
Own truth

If the Dear
Offers universal
Justice, peace and
Cooperative spirit
In that case, His
Reality is validated
Of course

Otherwise,
The historic fate
Leaves something
To be desired of the
Holy invention...

Epicenter

The "Self"
What a fragile
Gift demanding
Strong conduct
Always

"Self" the
Very essence
Asking
To gather-up
Intuitive spirit
Before it's too late

"Self,"
Asking,
"How to
Take care of it
Before its no
Longer the
Experience"

"Self"
What a gift of
Courage casting
Light over the
Dark terrain...

Common Sense

Only
Simplicity
Shall give us
Freedom

Only
Compassion
Shall turn
Our dream into
Reality in time

Yes,
That s how
Simple,
The reward of
Existence is all
About

We the,
"Intelligent"
Shouldn't be
Aware of
Such strength of
A simple truth!

Good Morning!

If we
Know our
Possibilities
We
Shall write
The grand story
And be
Vindicated in
The end

If
We're the
Determined
Wills
We
Shall make it
Through all the
Way to the
Set mission...

New
Image

Let's
Arrive at a
Historic milestone,
And ask,
"Having absolved
All our blunders
And sins... are we
Ready to enter
The Temple of
Truth"

When
Glancing at
The mega mirror,
Of reality
Have we ever
Pondered,
"Are we walking
Along a right trail
Or not?"

Rule
101

Be sure
The tank is
Full of courage
And determined
Will to keep
Going for the
Journeys too long

That's
The Rule 101
For every daring
Being to remember
So well

That's
The truth
To know well
Before hitting
The pedal to
The realm called,
"Dream Come True"

Reality
As Is

Being and
Ambition
Two manifests
Of one reality
Only

Birth and
Death
Two ends of
One thread
Verily

Beauty and
Truth
Two jewels of
One inspiration,
Essentially

That's
The elegant
Harmony to be
Understood
With a simple
Ease...

The
Quest

God or
No-God,
Essence or
Existence...
Duality or
Non-duality
And so on

All dancing
Into the
Probing
Human mind

Each
Tackled with a
Kabuki dance
Through myths,
Beliefs and reason
Since the inception

Still the
Debate is on and
Truth seems too
Far even in this
Techno-Twenty-One!

Biography

Being
What a giant
Born with a
Long story of
His life and time

But the
Story keeps
Interrupted by
The vicissitude of
Existence;
Turning
Him Janus in
Many respects

And yet he
Remains an
Evolving
Perfection!

If that's the
Case, he's an
"Enlightened
Soul in-progress
Indeed"

Great
Circus

It's an
Impressive leap
Forward while
Knowing the inner
Being to the
Unknown cosmic
Realm

It's the
Very flow of
His creativity
Searching,
The meaning of
All there is called,
"Truth"

That is
When he
Becomes the
Eternal
Intelligent being
Himself..."

Task
Ahead

Where falsity,
Greed and
Solipsism remains
The main theme

In such a
State of the
Void,
"How shall we
Know,
"Who we're and
What we ought
To be"

At that
Point,
Existence
Seems to lost
Its charm and

We don't
Know yet
How to
Load it up with
Further
Common-sense!

Inheritors

We're
Ripples flowing
Through the crazy
Stream that
Can't find its
Way to the
Mighty Blue Sea

We're the
Poetic puzzles
Born with unity,
Simplicity and
Dignity, but
Can't find the
Right passage
To our own
Meaning

We're
Inheritors of
Good, but
Why then keep
Struggling so hard

Why not
Instead ask,
"Is there
Something missing
From the human
Equation or, what!"

In Love

When
In love,
We dance
With
Great joy

When
In love,
We also
Cry every
Night too

That's
The basic
Outcome of
Most lovers
Everywhere

That's
The story of
Crazy love
Always

Love
What a
Magic brining
Grief and joy,
To every heart,
Always...

A Gift

The Self
Wonderful
Essence of
Every being

The Self
What a gift
Called,
"Intuition"

The Self
What a
Great vision
To fulfill the
Noble mission

Yes
The Self,
The magnifique
Reality where
Million riddles still
Rule our experience...

The Drama

The drama
Of existence
Is a complex
Blend of many
Causes and
Consequences
Yet to be untied

If the
Choices made
Is right
There is a
Reward with
Every great
Forward stride

If not,
There is
Alienation,
Struggles and
Defeats waiting
In the wing

Be smart,
Be disciplined,
Be focused with
The right goals
For that's where
The real journey
Has a meaning...

Narrow
Gap

Before
Exploring
The world
We're after
We
Better
Read the
Stories of
Our heroes

Yes,
To strengthen
Our collective
Will to win the
Battle we're in

We
Better be
Aware of the
History,
"Every step
For good means
We're in eternal
Friction with the
Waiting evil"

Life
After Life

Dear
Beauty,
I invite you
To come and
Dance with me

Come and
Sing the song
To honor our
First meeting

So I say,
"Come and be
In love for the
First time"

Come
Dear heart
And dance to the
End of the time

For we're
In love... life
After life, after life
And there's never an
End to us to be, One...

Skin
To Skin

Silly
Madness of
"Skin to Skin
Difference"
Keeps
Spilling blood
And distrust even
In this intelligent
Twenty-One

As a
Consequence,
God, humanity,
Morality and the
Very dignity of us
Seems fading away
So fast

What
Happened
To our thoughts,
Wisdom and the
Common sense still
The big enigma of
Our intelligent
Twenty-One...

Being Measured

Journey
Begins and
Ends with a
Character of
Every being

It is the
Character
That paves
The right path

It is the
Individual
Who makes
Life worthy
And smart

While
On the stage
That is so brief...

Ahh, the Memories

Falling
In love,
Wedding,
Birth of
First one...
Graduation
And many more

So we write
The story called,
"Simply Us"

Yes to
Share with
Others while
Walking through
The thick and thin
Of our time

Reading
Each page
Reaffirms all
The trials and
Trepidations
We'd experienced
Since we arrived
On the blessed scene...

We
Exists

Every
Struggling
Being
Caught into the
Eternal flux
Of uncertainty
Alright

Every
Human seeking
His identity in
The dust storm
From where he
Can't escape

Yet every
Human
Striving to be
Good and know
His truth even
Trapped in such
A nasty place...

Mammoth Cave

What
A giant leap
Of miracle
From hunter
Gatherers to be
Techno- humans,
Today

Many
Millennia flew
In-between and
Million wars and
Blood spills left
Deep wounds behind

Sadly, the
Past memories
Keeps haunting
Modern beings
Who dwells
Into the
Mammoth cave

Where
Light is quite dim
And the dark still
Rules the place...

Lost, but Not Found

Being
Just a
Consequential
Passenger on a
Fast running
Train

He's
Pursuing the
Journey toward
A meaning that is
Still missing from
His thinking

Why is he
Standing
Still and why
Not proceed to
The set destiny

I mean,
Where
He can know
The value of
His own birth...

Flashers

Do we?
Dare go from
Ordinary to be the
Spiritual giant or
Not?

That is the
Question keeps
Revolving
While searching
The teasing truth

Do we?
Dare go from
Being fearful to be
The fearless giant or
Not?

Is that the
Question be
Revolving against
The false narratives
And blind belief or
What?

Courage
To Be

Being
Alone is the
Very reflection of
Moral intention and
Rational orientation
While in the quest of
His personal truth

Don't let him
Bury beneath the
Imperfections of
All that is

Don't let him
Be fearful and
Succumb to the
Pseudo-beliefs and
Dried-up dreams

Let him
Inspire young
Let him offer
Confidence and
Courage to manage
Their contextual
Experience well...

Immortals

We're
Young forever
Yes,
Sweetheart,
We're born to
Be in love 'til
The light is
In the universe

That is
Our immortal
Will and
That is the
Truth of
Our friendship

Yes,
Sweetheart
That is the way
That is the
Very meaning of
Our love to be
As always...

Be Happy

So I say,
"Come and be
Mine for no point
Waiting in the line
For happiness"

Ignore the
Dark days just
Come and dance
With me one more
Time

I say,
"Let's celebrate
The moments
We're
Sharing today"

Ignore the
Gray clouds
And be mine and
Enjoy the smile
Again

I say,
"Just keep
Dancing to be
Forever..."

Toward Perfection!

One day,
Transcendental
Experience shall
Clarify all the
Persuasions

If
That turns
Out to be
The genuine
Human
Awakening

Let
The journey
Continue with
Full gusto and
Great vision

Whatever
The prospects,
Let life keep
Rolling and
Never
To be an empty
Experience...

Being:
In-
Progress

While
Spinning
Into this
Whirlpool
Full of
Debates and
Doubts

Many
Unknowns
Still to be
Understood
Through the
Rational mind

And never
To ignore the
Moral intention
At the same time

Let us
Be the
"Witnessing
Consciousness"
To all that is...

Contagion

Existence,
Why
Stigmatized
It
Time after
Time

Why be
Suspended into
Doom and
Gloom to
Report

Is it
'Cause
We're the
Disease called,
"Greed, falsity
And narcissism
Or whatever"

Why not
Relearn to
Govern
The nasty old
Habits of the
Corrupted mind...

Light & Shadow

No matter
How
We slice it,
Every being
Often a shadow
To his own light

When
Leaving the
Safety of the
Cave
Man took a
Giant leap
And became the
Master of the
Universe

The present
Calls for
Another such
A magic leap
To reinvigorate
His moral inner
Being...

Let's
Rock'n Roll

Hey Babe
Jump-up from
Despair and

Come
To my world
To salute this
Magic
Name, "Love"

Hey, hey
Babe don't
Run away from
Life's funs... come
And rock 'n roll
Tonight

Be brave
And fall in
Love with a
Vigor of your
Full heart
Tonight

Come on
Babe just
Rock 'n roll with
All the joy your
Heart can hold
Tonight ...

Affirmation

Let's
Gather our
Total strength
And soar to
Higher and
Higher than
We ever
Imagined

That's
The goal and
That's the
Determination
To go beyond
Where we're
Forever

Let's
Put in action
Our will to win
And keep
Ascending higher
And higher than
We've ever reckoned
Our amazing strength...

Be
Smart

Only
Way to
Repair brain
Damage is
To gain
Higher powers
Of tolerance and
Stop committing
Sins so willingly

Only
Way to
Avoid saying,
"Sorry" is to kill
Ignorance at once

Only
Way to be
Smart is to know,
"How to talk less
And listen to others,
What they got
To say in return..."

Silhouette

I dwell
Into this
Grand matrix

Where all is
Ephemeral and
Subject to death

And where
'Am always
Between my
Imperfection
And perfection
Yet to be

Wonder,
In such
An uncertain
World,

"What is the
Value of my belief,
My mission and
My very essence?"

Third
Eye

Through
The Third Eye
I remain
Conscious of the
Self and the
Surrounding world
I've began to know

Through its
Very vision,
I keep walking
With my
Full alacrity and
Optimism to grasp
The power within

In such a
Glorious milieu
Let I dare roll from
Impossibilities to
Possibilities not as
A dream but the
Reality that I must...

The Game

Our
Individual
Life is an
Open book
For it lacks
The big
Surprises
Any more

Our
Fears are
Same but we
Hid 'em
Differently at
Every stage of
Existence

Our wishes
Are same but
We express 'em
Differently to prove
The silent arrogance

Our feelings
Of love is
Universal, but
The consequences
Often are not the same...

Riders

We're
Creative
Riders of the
Ever evolving life

We keep
Flying through
Million waiting
Dreams to turn
Them into reality,
At once

While
In the flight,
"We're
All equals as
We try to
Survive on this
Fragile Planet by
The passing minute

We've no
Choice for the
Rides so uncertain
And poked with
Many thorns and
Not enough roses
To keep the spirits
Going...

Walkers

It is
Believed,
"Trials and
Errors must be
The way to
Human Wisdom"

It is also
Understood,
"Grief and joy
Is the
Consequence
Of existence"

We got
No choice,
But to keep
Walking,
Walking and
Walking 'til we
Know,

"How to
Wake-up and
Act to secure
Our only truth."

"I"

What I
Think and
What I say
Sometimes
Don't
Come out
The same in
Meaning

What I
Say and
What others
Grasps may
Not be the same
In the message

Sometimes,
What I
Write and what
Readers may
Interpret may
Not be in sync

But then
That's where
Begins a greater
Awareness:
Controversy,
Criticism and out
Right disgust!

Ascension

We the
Intelligent
Beings
Living off a
Borrowed time
And we keep
Looking for
Truth, but we're
Not there yet

We're
Inventors of
Myriad riddles:
Life, God and
The Universe,
But no luck yet
To get
The real answer

We're
The temporal
Searching,
"How to be
Eternals," and
The pursuit remains
Still inconclusive...

Harmony

After
Exploring
Million pages
Of history
Have we ever
Thought

It's in the
Individual
Moral Self
Where
Harmony and
Happiness
Resides!

Did we ever
Care to take
Note that the
Unity of the
Whole where
Our collective
Truth hides!"

The Passage

Do grasp
Essence of the
Inner being and
Begin the ascend
To the distant stars
And say, "Hello to
Truth for the first
Time"

Be sure to
Inspire the young
Braves to ride along
The highway named,
"Compassion,
Harmony & Hope"

Let 'em
Know the
Noble goal of
Their births well

Let 'em be the
Spiritual beings
To move the world
For the first time"

Great
Wait

While
Gazing at the
Brilliance of
This majestic
Universe

Wonder,
"Why its
So illumined
With beauty
And grace and
The petite being
Ain't?"

Why
All that flow
Of radiating
Grandeur not
Granted him to be
The Perfect Being!

Recollections

Oh the
Rhythms of the
On-coming waves
Bringing in
All the vigor
From the mighty
Blue Sea

In such an
Inspiration,
The soul unveiled
Meaning of my
Own being,

But the
Thunders and
Lightning
Interrupted
It all

And here
I am, striving
To recover all
That once I'd in
My deep experience...

Unfolding

Where
Ideas and
Reality becomes
One at that
Turning point,
Being is an
Awakened
Spirit indeed

There
Must be the
Presence of
His Perfection
Driving him to
Arrive at such a
State of the mind

Where
Unity of
Wholeness is
The fact of life
And where
Inspiration
Is eternal

That is where
Pragmatic human
Shall know the value
Of his awakened
Inner Being in time...

Still on
The Run

Being,
What a
Run away
Empirical
Experience

Always
Keeps asking:
Validation of
God,
Immortality,
Will and so on

Being,
What an
Existential
Enigma to be
Understood
Fully well,
Even today!

Modern Human

Being
Who's
A part of
Nature should
Be the solemn
Spirit, but
Why he's not?

What a
Reality to
Confront while
All is so mighty
Unity, but

The
Modern beings
Seem to be
Disintegrating
Into myopia, phobia,
Tribalism and more....

Don't
Wait

Dear Heart
Come and
Celebrate
Joy of
Two humans
In love for the
First time

Love
What an elixir
Showering upon
Our waiting feelings

Don't
Wait and don't
Pretend to be a
Stranger every time

For our feelings
Have merged and
Nowhere to hide
But to fall in love,
At once for the
First time ...

Meditative
Magic

Flying
Away from
The world of
Nothing is the
First thought

That keeps
Revolving
Now and then
Always in the
Mind

It's
A wonderful
Poetic Bliss
Hovering over
My very
Human essence

I say,
"Let the
Poetica
All in all be
Catharsis to
My searching
Soul for sure."

World Today

Darkness
Destroys
Begnin dream

Darkness
Prevails when
Folks fail to
Know their
Moral sense

Darkness
Never
Goes away
When lies,
Corruptions and
Tribalism rules
The gullible beings...

JAGDISH J. BHATT, PhD
(Retired- Professor) brings 45
years of academic experience and the
authorship of 45 books which cover
the scientific and the literary fields.

Made in the USA
Columbia, SC
14 May 2022